Symphony No. 1
in D Major
("Titan")

Gustav Mahler

DOVER PUBLICATIONS, INC.
Mineola, New York

Copyright

Published in Canada by General Publishing Company, Ltd., 30 Lesmill
Road, Don Mills, Toronto, Ontario.
Published in the United Kingdom by Constable and Company, Ltd., 3 The
Lanchesters, 162–164 Fulham Palace Road, London W6 9ER.

Bibliographical Note

This Dover edition, first published in 1998, is a republication of *Erste
Symphonie in D dur,* originally published by Josef Weinberger, Vienna, n.d.
[1899]. The glossary, background note, and lists of contents and instrumen-
tation are newly added.

International Standard Book Number: 0-486-40419-6

Manufactured in the United States of America
Dover Publications, Inc., 31 East 2nd Street, Mineola, N.Y. 11501

The work that was to become Mahler's Symphony No. 1 was first performed as a symphonic poem in two parts and five movements. 'Blumine', the original *andante* movement, was later discarded. The composition was begun about 1884, completed in 1888, and published by Josef Weinberger the following year; the present edition is a republication of that score. Between 1893 and 1896, Mahler prepared a lightly revised version—consisting mostly of minor reorchestrations in the last movement—that was published by Universal Edition in 1906.

Programmatic and personalized in the general manner of Richard Strauss's tone poems, Mahler's symphony opens with a movement built on the song "Gieng heut' Morgen über's Feld" (I went out this morning over the countryside) from his cycle *Lieder eines fahrenden Gesellen* (Songs of a Wayfarer). The funeral-march third movement—a folk-music parody—quotes the song "Die zwei blauen Augen" (The two blue eyes) from the same cycle. The title "Titan" is Mahler's own.

CONTENTS

Symphony No. 1
in D Major, "Titan"

GLOSSARY

(The words appear here exactly as they appear in the score.)

ab, off
abdämpfen, damp
aber, but
abnehmend, waning
abreissen, break off, flag
alle(s), all
allmählich, gradually
als, like, than
alten, old
am, at the
an, to
andern, others
Anfang(e), beginning
Anfangstempo, opening tempo
angebunden, played at the same time
Anmerkung, note
anmuthig, gracefully
anschwellend, crescendo
anzuschlagen, to be struck
As, A♭
auf, on, for
aufgeboh., aufgeh., aufg., raised
aufgestellt, placed
aus, from
(sich) ausbreitend, broadening out
Ausdruck, expression
ausdrucksvoll, expressively
ausgeführt, played
auszuhalten, to sustain
B, B♭
Bässe, double basses
bedächtig, deliberate
befestigt, attached
beginnen, begin
behaglich, comfortable
bei, on
beide, both
beinahe, almost
besonders, especially
Betonungen, accentuation
bewegt, animated, agitated
bewegter, più mosso
Bewegung, motion, tempo
bezeichneten, marked
bis zum, until the
bitterlich, bitterly
bleiben, remain, *bleibt*, remains
Bogen, bow
brechen, arpeggiate
breit, broad, broadly, *breiter*, more broadly
Celli, cellos

Cis, C♯
Consonanten, consonant
Dämpfer, mute, mutes, muting
das, the
dasselbe, the same
dem, den, the
der, the, of the, who
Des, D♭
deutlich, clearly
die, the
diesen, this
Dirigenten, conductor
dirigiren, conduct, beat
doch, but
Doppelgriff, Dopplgr., double stop
drängend, pressing, *drängender*, more pressing
dumpf, muffled, dull
durch, (obtained) through
durchaus, throughout
eben, just previously
ebenfalls, likewise
ebenso, just as
Echoton, echo tone
edlen, noble, exalted
eilen, hurry, *ohne zu .eilen*, without hurrying
eilend, hurrying
eine, einem, a, one (player)
einer, eines, of a
einige, several
(sich) entfernend, becoming distant
Entfernung, distance
Empfindung, feeling, emotion
empfunden, (deeply) felt
entschieden, resolute
erste(n), first
ersterbend, dying away
Es, E♭
etwas, somewhat
Ferne, distance
feurige, fiery
Fidel, medieval fiddle
Figuren, figures
Fis, F♯
Flag., harmonics
fliessend, flowing
folgend, following, in keeping with
fort, continuing
fortlaufend(er), running, continuous
frei, freely
freihängend, suspended
frisch, vigorous, lively
früher, earlier
für, for

furchtbarer, formidable
ganzes, full
ganzlich, completely
gebrochen, arpeggiated
gebunden, legato
gedämpft, damped
gedehnt, drawn out
gehalten(en), held, held back, meno mosso
gehaltener, more restrained
geheimnisvoll(er), mysterious
gehen, go
gemächlich, comodo, easily, *gemächlicher*, più comodo
gemässigt(e), moderate
geringste, briefest
gerissen, cut off
Ges, G♭
gesangvoll, cantabile
gesättigten, saturated
geschlagen, struck
gestimmt, tuned
gestopft, gest., stopped
gestrichen, bowed
gesungen, sung
getheilt, geth., divisi
getragen, solemn
Gewalt, power
gewirbelt, rolled
gewöhnlich(e), ordinario, normally
Gis, G♯
gleichen, equal-sized
gleichmässiger, even
grell, shrill
Gr. Fl., flute
Griffbrett, fingerboard, sul tasto
grob, coarsely, rudely
grossem, grosser, great, large
grössere, larger
gut, quite
H, B
Halbe, (beat in) half-notes
Hälfte, half (of a string section)
Halt, pause
hart, hard
Hast, haste
Haupttempo, principal tempo
Hauptzeitmass, principal tempo
herausgestossen, thrust out
hervortretend, hervortr., prominently
hier, here, *von hier an*, from here on
hinaufziehen, approaching from below
hinunterziehen, approaching from above
hoch, high

iv

höchster, greatest
hohe, high
Höhe, elevation, *in die Höhe, i. d. Höhe*, up, in the air
höher, higher
Holzbläser, woodwinds
Holzschlägeln, wooden mallets
hörbar, audible
im, in, in the
immer, always
ja, absolutely
kaum, barely
keck, bold
keine, no
klagend, lamenting
Klang, sound
kleine, small
klingen, ring
klingt, sounds
Kopfstimme, head voice
Kraft, Kraftentfaltung, power
kräftig, robustly
kurz(er), short
Lage, position
lange, long
langhallenden, long-resounding
langsam, slow, *langsamer*, slower
(sich) lassen, allow
lebhaft, lively
leidenschaftlich, passionately
leise, softly
letzten, previous
lustig, merry, merrily
Marsch, march
mehr, more
mehrfach besetzt, several to a part
merklich, noticeably
mit, with
mittlere, medium, middle
möglich, possible
möglichst, as . . . as possible
munter, cheerfully
Musiker, musician
nach, (retune) to
nachgeben, broaden
nachhorchend, listening
nachlassen, relax
Nachschlag, Nachschl., turn (at end of trill)
nachzuahmen, to imitate
(sich) nähernd, drawing nearer
Naturlaut, sound of nature
natürlich, ordinario
nehmen, take, change to
nicht, not, don't
nimmt, take, change to
noch, still
Note, notes
Notfall, necessity, *nur im Notfall zur*, only if necessary for
nur, only
offen, open, unstopped
ohne, without
Oktav(e), octave

Orchester, orchestra
Piston, cornet, *kleinem Piston*, small cornet in E♭
plötzlich, suddenly, *plözlichem*, sudden
Pralltriller, mordents
Pulte, desks, stands
recht, quite, very
Rhythmus, rhythm
roh(er), rough, crude
Rücksicht, regard
ruhevoll, peaceful
ruhig, calm
Saite, string
sanft, soft
Satz, movement
Schalltrichter, Schalltr., bells (of wind instruments)
Schlägeln, mallets
schlagen, beat, conduct
schleppen, drag
Schluss, end
schmetternd, blaring, resounding
schnell, fast, *schneller*, faster
Schwammschlägeln, sponge mallets
schwer, heavy
Schwung, energy
schwungvoll, energetically
sehr, very
selben, same
singend, singing
so . . . als, as . . . as
sofort, immediately
Sordinen, mutes
Spieler, players, *2. Spieler*, second group of 1st violins
spring. Bog., sautillé
stark, strongly, *stärker*, stronger, *stärker besetzt*, more players to a part
Steg, bridge
steigernd, intensifying
Steigerungen, increases
stetig, stets, steadily
Stimme, voice, group of 1st violins
Streicher, strings
streng, strictly
Strich, bowstroke, *Strich für Strich*, one bow per note, détaché
stürmen, rage, rush
summend, humming
Takt, beat, time
taktiren, tactiren, conduct, beat
Tellern, mit Tellern, clashed cymbals
Tempowechsel, change in tempo
Theilen, sections
tief(e), low, *tiefer*, lower
Ton, note, tone, sonority
Tönen, notes
Tonhöhe, register
Triangelschlägel, triangle beater
Triller, trill
Triolen, triplets
über, over, *über das ganze Orchester hinaus*, rising above the whole orchestra

Übergange, transition
übernimmt, takes, changes to
überraschend, surprisingly
übertönend, rising above, *alles übertönend*, louder than the rest of the orchestra
und, and
ungefähr, approximately
unmerklich, imperceptibly
Unterstützung, reinforcement, support
verändern, changing
verdoppelt, doubled
verhallend, becoming fainter
verklingend, dying away
Verlaufe, course
(sich) verlierend, dying away
Vermittlung, transition
verschwindend, disappearing
versehen, provided
versieht, plays
vibrirend, vibrating, with vibrato
viel, much, a lot of
Viertel, quarter-notes
Vokal, vowel
vollziehen, execute, *vollzieht sich*, to be executed
vom, by the
von, by
vorgetragen, played
vorhanden, (is) available
vorher, vorhin, before
Vorschläge, grace notes
vorwärts, pressing forward
wechseln, change
weich, soft, gently
Weise, tune, call
weiter, far, *weitester*, farthest
welche, which
wenig, little
wenn, if
werden, becoming
wie, as, as though
wieder, again
wild, unrestrained
womöglich, wo möglich, if possible
Worte, words
wuchtiger, more heavily, more vigorously
zart(e), gentle, gently, tenderly
Zeit, time
zögernd, hesitating
zu, to, in, at, *zu 2, 3, 4*, unisono
zuerst, at first
zufahrend, pressing, stringendo
zuletzt, just previously
zum, zur, to the
zurückhalten(d), meno mosso, *zurückhaltender*, more restrained
zurückkehren, return, *zurückkehrend*, returning
zwei, two
1., 2., 3., 4., 1st, 2nd, 3rd, 4th
2te, 3te, 4te, 2nd, 3rd, 4th
2(3,4) fach, in 2(3,4) parts

INSTRUMENTATION

4 Flutes [Flöte, Fl.], two alternating on
  2 Piccolos [Piccolo, Picc.]
4 Oboes [Oboe, Ob.], one alternating on
  English Horn [Engl. Horn]
4 Clarinets [Clarinette, Clar.] (B♭, C, E♭, A), one alternating on
  Bass Clarinet [Bass-Clarinette, Basscl.] (B♭)—"doubled at least"
  in last movement
3 Bassoons [Fagott, Fag.], one alternating on
  Contrabassoon [Contra-Fagott, Contrafag.]

7 Horns [Horn] (F), with "reinforcement" in last movement
4 Trumpets [Trompete, Trmp.] (F, B♭), with added Trumpet in last
  movement
3 Trombones [Posaune, Pos.]
Tuba [Tuba]

4 Timpani [Pauken] (2 players)
Cymbals [Becken]
Triangle [Triangel]
Tam-tam [Tam-Tam]
Bass Drum [Grosse Trommel, Gr. Tr.]

Harp [Harfe]

Violins [Violine, Viol.] I, II
Violas [Viola]
Cellos [Violoncello, Cello]
Basses [Contrabass, Bass]

Symphony No. 1
in D Major, "Titan"

1

* Hier ist nach allmählicher Steigerung ein frisches, belebtes Zeitmass eingetreten.
(♩ = 116)

* Hier ist nach allmählicher Steigerung ein frisches, belebtes Zeitmass eingetreten.
(♩ = 116)

* Hier ist nach allmählicher Steigerung ein frisches, belebtes Zeitmass eingetreten.
(♩ = 116)

18

263

19

312

ppp Beginn der Steigerung. Celli, Bässe, Fag. 3. Pos. u. Tuba etwas hervortretend
Immer noch etwas zurück
25
335
langsames crescendo
Piccolo
zu 2
1.2. Fl. 3.
1.2. Ob. 3.
1.2. in B Clar. 4. in Es
1.2. Fag.
Contrafag.
1.3. Horn 2.4.
1.2. Trmp.
3. Pos. Tuba
Gr. Tr.
1. Viol.
2. Viol.
Viola
Cello
Bass
poco a poco cresc.
geth.
subito
trem.
2. Violinen ohne crescendo
Aumerkung für den Dirigenten: 1. Geigen crescendo
2. Geigen ohne crescendo
Immer noch etwas zurück

Von hier ab wird das Tempo bis zum Zeichen ⊖ in unmerklicher, aber stetiger Steigerung immer lebhafter.

Von hier ab wird das Tempo bis zum Zeichen ⊖ in unmerklicher, aber stetiger Steigerung immer lebhafter.

Von hier ab wird das Tempo bis zum Zeichen ⊖ in unmerklicher, aber stetiger Steigerung immer lebhafter.

440
Schnell (bis zum Schluss)
G.P.
zu 3
zu 2
sempre stacc.
gestopft
mit Sord.
arco
geth
1.2.3.Fl.
Ob.
Clar.
Fag.
Horn
Trmp.
1.2.Pos.
3.Pos. Tuba
Pauke
Triangel
1.Viol.
2.Viol.
Viola
Cello
Bass

42
5
1.2. Fl. 3.
1.2. Ob. 3.
1.2. Clar. 3.
1.2. Fag. 3.
1.2. Horn 3.4. Horn 5.6. Horn 7.
1.2. Trp.
1 Viol.
2 Viol.
Viola
Cello
Bass
zu 2
Schalltrichter in die Höhe!
Schalltr. auf!
gestopft
geth.
pizz.
ff
mf
p
5

6

31
Vorwärts.
Vorwärts.
32
339
1.2. Fl. 3.
zu 2
1.2. Ob. 3.
1. Clar. 2.3.
1.2. Fag. 3.
1.2. Horn 3.4.
Horn 5.
Horn 6.7.
1.2. Trmp.
Pauke
1.Viol.
2.Viol.
Viola
Cello
Bass
cresc.
geth.
pizz.
Vorwärts.
31
Vorwärts.
32

349
accelerando al Fine.
Ganzes Orchester
scharf abreissen.
1.2. Fl. 3.
1.2. Ob. 3.
1. Clar. 2.3.
1. Fag. 2.3.
1.2. Horn 3.4.
Horn 5.6.7.
1.2. Trmp. 3.4.
1.2. Pos.
3. Pos. Tuba
Triangel
Becken
Pauke
1. Viol.
2. Viol.
Viola
Cello
Bass
zu 2
zu 3
mit der untern Note trillern
schnell abdämpfen
arco
accelerando al Fine.
Hier eine ziemliche Pause machen,
bevor der nächste Satz (No.3.) beginnt.

3

87

14

*) Anmerkung für den Dirigenten: Kein Irrthum! Mit dem Holz zu streichen.

Folgt sogleich № 4.

93

3

68

76

107
1.2. Fl.
1.4. Oboe 2.3.
1. Clar. in C 2.3.
1.2. Fag. 3.
1.2. Horn 3.4. Horn 5.6. Horn 7.
1.2. Trmp. 3.4.
1.2. Pos.
3. Pos. und Tuba
1. Pauker
Becken
Gr. Tr.
1. Viol. 2.
Viola
Cello
Bass
zu 2
molto cresc.
gest.
offen
mit Schwammschlägel
poco cresc.
cresc.

114
10
1.2. Picc.
1.2. Fl.
1.4.
Oboe
2.3.
1. in C.
Clar.
2.3.
Clar.
4. in Es
1.2.
Fag.
3.
1.2.
Horn
3.4.
Horn
5.6.
Horn
7
offen
1.2.
Trmp.
3.4.
1.2. Pos.
3. Pos. und Tuba
1. Pauker
Gr. Tr.
1.
Viol.
2.
Viola
Cello
Bass
zu 2
ff
f
fp
10

121
1.2. Fl.
1.4.
Oboe
2.3.
1.in C
Clar.
2.3.
Clar.
4.in Es
1.2.
Fag.
3.
1.2.
Horn
3.4.
Horn
5.6.
Horn
7.
1.2.
Trmp.
3.4.
1.2.Pos.
3.Pos.
und
Tuba
1.
Pauker
2.
Gr. Tr.
1.
Viol.
2.
Viola
Cello
Bass
zu 2

128
1.2.Picc.
1.2.Fl.
1. Oboe
2.3. Oboe
4.
1.in C Clar.
2.3. Clar.
4.in Es
1.2. Fag.
3.
1.2. Horn
3.4. Horn
5.6.
1.2. Trmp.
3.4.
1.2.Pos.
3.Pos. und Tuba
1. Pauker
2.
1. Viol.
2.
Viol.
Cello
Bass

135
11
1.2. Picc.
1.2. Fl.
1. Oboe 2.3. Oboe 4.
1. in C Clar. 2.3. Clar. 4. in Es
1.2. Fag. 3.
1.2. Horn 3.4. Horn 5.6.
1.2. Trmp.
1.2. Pos.
1. Pauker 2.
1. Viol. 2.
Viola
Cello
Bass
zu 2
geth.
ff
fp
f
11

346

Anmerkung für den Dirigenten: Die Betonungen *fp* in den Violen, Celli u. Bässen sowie auch in den andern Instrumenten werden entsprechend dem allgemeinen Diminuendo immer schwächer und schwächer ausgeführt.

Steigerung! Langsam steigern!
609
Zurückhaltend
4. Picc.
1.2. Fl.
1.2.3. Obor 4.
1.2.3. in C Clar. 4. in Es
1. Fag. 2.3.
1.3. Horn 2.4.
1.3. Trmp. 2.4.
1.2. Pos.
Gr. Tr.
1. Viol. 2.
Viola
Cello
Bass
zu 2
zu 3
poco a poco cresc.
sempre p
pp Die ^ werden allmählich stärker und stärker bis zum
fp
f
Steigerung! Langsam steigern!
Zurückhaltend

Poco rit.
Pesante.
53 Vorwärts.
628
ohne Nachschlag
zu 2
zu 4
zu 3
stacc.
1.2. Picc.
1.2. Fl.
1.2.3.4. Oboe
1.2.3. in C Clar.
4. in Es
1. Fag. 2.3.
1.2. Horn
3.4. Horn
5.6. Horn
7.
1.2. Trmp. 3.4.
1.2. Pos.
3. Pos. und Tuba
Triangel
1. Pauker 2.
Gr. Tr.
1. Viol. 2.
Viola
Cello
Bass

639
54
1.2. Picc.
1.2. Fl.
zu 3
1.2.3.
Ob.
4.
1.2.3.
in C
Clar.
4. in Es
1.2.3. Fag.
1.2.
Horn
3.4.
Horn
5.6.
Horn
7.
zu 2
1.2.
Trmp.
3.4.
1.2.
Pos.
3.
1.
Pauker
2.
Triangel
1. Viol.
2. Viol.
Viola.
Cello.
Bass.
54

691
59
1.2. Picc.
1.2. Fl.
1.4. Ob. 2.3.
1.2. in C Clar. 3. in C
Cla. 4. in Es
1. Fag. 2.3.
1.3.5.6. Horn 2.4.7.
Hörner Verstärkg.
1.2. Trmp. 3.4.
1.2. Pos.
3. Pos. Tuba.
1. Pauker 2.
Triangel
Becken
1. Viol. 2.
Viola
Cello
Bass
zu 2
zu 4
zu 3
59

699
1.2. Fl.
2.3.4. Ob.
1.2. in C Clar.
3. in C Clar.
4. in Es
1. Fag.
2. 3.
1.2. Horn
3.4. Horn
5.6. Horn
7.
Hörner Verstkng.
1.2. Trmp.
3.4.
1.2. Pos.
3. Pos. Tuba
1. Pauker
2.
Triangel
Becken
Gr. Tr.
1. Viol.
2.
Viola
Cello
Bass
zu 2
zu 4

716
1.2.Picc.
1.2.Fl.
1.4. Ob. 2.3.
1.2.in C Clar.
3.in C Clar.
4.in Es
1.2. Fag. 3.
Hörner-Verstärkung unisono mit 1. und 2. Horn.
1.2. Horn
3.4. Horn
5.6. Horn
7.
1.2. Trmp. 3.4.
1.2.Pos.
3.Pos. Tuba
1. Pauker 2.
Becken
Triangel
1. Viol. 2.
Viola
Cello
Bass
zu 2
ffp
ff
tr

END OF EDITION